D1462889

A Special Gift

FOR:

_____

FROM:

_____

DATE:

_____

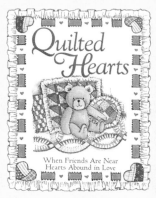

Quilted Hearts

When Friends Are Near
Hearts Abound in Love

Illustrated by: Holly Jo Camp

Brownlow

Brownlow Publishing Company, Inc.

Little Treasures
Miniature Books

A Little Cup of Tea

All Things Great & Small

Angels of Friendship

Baby's First Book of Angels

Baby's First Little Bible

Cherished Bible Stories

Dear Teacher

Faith

Faithful Friends

Flowers of Graduation

For My Secret Pal

From Friend to Friend

Grandmothers Are for Loving

Hope

Love

Mother

My Sister, My Friend

Precious Are the Promises

Quilted Hearts

Soft as the Voice of an Angel

The Night the Angels Sang

Contents

CHAPTER ONE
Life Is...

CHAPTER TWO
Faith for Living

CHAPTER THREE
Wisdom for Today

CHAPTER FOUR
The Way of Love

CHAPTER FIVE
A Cheerful Heart

Life is not so short
but that there is always
time for courtesy.

RALPH WALDO EMERSON

Our necessities are few
but our wants are endless.

H. W. SHAW

In the long run, we shape
our lives, and we shape ourselves.
The process never ends until we die.
And the choices we make are
ultimately our own responsibility.

ELEANOR ROOSEVELT

There are no birds this year
in last year's nest.

ITALIAN PROVERB

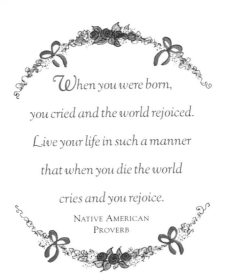

When you were born,

you cried and the world rejoiced.

Live your life in such a manner

that when you die the world

cries and you rejoice.

NATIVE AMERICAN
PROVERB

Life is a coin. You can
spend it any way you wish,
but you can spend it only once.

LILLIAN DICKSON

Few things are harder to put up
with than a good example.

MARK TWAIN

When a man is going to
try to borrow money it is
wise to look prosperous.

BENJAMIN DISRAELI

Some persons think they have
made a success of life when
all they have made is money.

ANONYMOUS

If it weren't for the last minute,
nothing would get done.

UNKNOWN

An intellectual is someone
who can listen to the
"William Tell Overture" without
thinking of the Lone Ranger.

A day

of worry is

more exhausting

than a week

of work.

The secret of life is not
to do what one likes,
but to try to like
what one has to do.

Opportunities are usually
disguised as hard work,
so most people
don't recognize them.

If at first
you *do* succeed,
try to hide
your astonishment.

*Y*ou can't turn
back the clock,
but you can
wind it up again.

The Roses of Today

One of the most tragic things I know about human nature is that all of us tend to put off living. We are all dreaming of some magical rose garden over the horizon—instead of enjoying the roses that are blooming outside our windows today.

DALE CARNEGIE

Nothing is quite so annoying
as to have someone
go right on talking
when you are interrupting.

Cosmetics were used in
the Middle Ages; in fact
they're still used in
the Middle Ages.

We do not know what to do
with this short life, yet we want
another which will be eternal.

ANATOLE FRANCE

It is a funny thing about life;
if you refuse to accept
anything but the best,
you very often get it.

W. SOMERSET MAUGHAM

They say garbage can be made
into gasoline—and why not!
It's already being made into
movies, books, and TV shows.

ABBOTT'S JOURNAL

Don't wait for a crisis
to discover what is
important in your life.

Living means making your life
a memorable experience.

The rooster may
strut and crow, but it's the
hen that delivers the goods.

A diet is a short period
of starvation followed by
a gain of five pounds.

There are only two kinds
of people who fail:
those who listen to
nobody and those who
listen to everybody.

A great man is always
willing to be little.

RALPH WALDO EMERSON

CHAPTER TWO
Faith for Living

*Faith makes things
possible – not easy.*

*God tempers the wind
to the shorn lamb.*

ENGLISH PROVERB

After crosses and losses,
men grow humbler and wiser.

BENJAMIN FRANKLIN

Dear God, help me get me up;
I can fall down by myself.

Tall trees catch much wind.

I am only one,

But still I am one.

I cannot do everything,

But still I can do something;

And because I

cannot do everything

I will not refuse to do

the something that I can do.

EDWARD EVERETT HALE

We have committed
the Golden Rule to memory.
Let us now commit it to life.

ANONYMOUS

God knows well which
are the best pilgrims.

ENGLISH PROVERB

He that does what he can
does what he ought.

Spring

If spring came but once in a century instead of once a year, or burst forth with the sound of an earthquake, and not in silence, what wonder and expectation there would be in all hearts to behold the miraculous change.

HENRY WADSWORTH LONGFELLOW

God does not take away
the darkness, but He
guides us through it.

The treasures which are
kept in coffers are not real,
but only those which
are kept in the soul.

ALEXANDER MACLAREN

Men do not attract
that which they want, but
that which they are.

JAMES ALLEN

Our fidelity will not be
without failures, nor our
confidences without fears.

THOMAS LYNCH

God cares for people,
through people.

You must plow with
such oxen as you have.

ENGLISH PROVERB

The real voyage of discovery
consists not in seeking
new landscapes, but in
having new eyes.

MARCEL PROUST

God gives the nuts, but
He does not crack them.

OLD PROVERB

It wasn't raining
when Noah built the ark.

HOWARD RUFF

He that would have the fruit
must climb the tree.

ENGLISH PROVERB

Our lives

are a

manifestation

of what

we think

about God.

The light of God surrounds me.
The love of God enfolds me.
The power of God protects me.
The presence of God
watches over me.
Wherever I am, God is.

Somebody figured it out—we
have 35 million laws to enforce
the ten commandments.

Two marks of a holy person:
giving and forgiving.

God gives every bird his food,
but He does not throw it
into the nest.

JOSIAH GILBERT HOLLAND

When we forget ourselves,
we usually do something that
everyone else remembers.

The great act of faith is when man
decides that he is not God.

O. W. HOLMES, JR.

The handsomest flower is not
always the sweetest.

CHAPTER THREE
Wisdom for Today

Obstacles are those frightful
things you see when you take
your eyes off the goal.

HANNAH MOORE

Before you can score
you must first have a goal.

GREEK PROVERB

With some people even their
roosters seem to lay eggs.

RUSSIAN PROVERB

Our incomes are like shoes:
if too small, they pinch;
if too large, we stumble.

COLTON

Every bird must
hatch her own eggs.

We must sow even
after a bad harvest.
DANISH PROVERB

The heart has no secret
which our conduct
does not reveal.
FRENCH PROVERB

Running down people
is a bad habit,
whether you are
a gossip or a motorist.

Let us be thankful for the fools.
But for them the rest of us
could not succeed.

MARK TWAIN

The dog with the bone
is always in danger.

AMERICAN PROVERB

If things go wrong,
don't go with them.

ROGER BABSON

They hurt themselves
that wrong others.

'Tis easy enough
to be pleasant,
When life flows along
like a song;
But the man worth while
Is the one who will smile
When everything
goes dead wrong.

ELLA WHEELER
WILCOX

A good name keeps
its luster in the dark.

Don't tell me that worry
doesn't do any good. The things
I worry about don't happen.

I am not everybody's dog
that whistles.

The way to gain
a good reputation is to
endeavor to be what
you desire to appear.

SOCRATES

We can better
appreciate the miracle
of a sunrise if we have
waited in darkness.

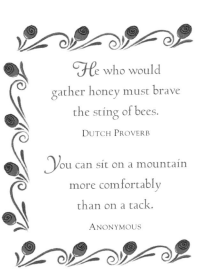

He who would
gather honey must brave
the sting of bees.

DUTCH PROVERB

You can sit on a mountain
more comfortably
than on a tack.

ANONYMOUS

In times like these,
it helps to recall that
there have always been
times like these.

PAUL HARVEY

If your head is wax,
don't walk in the sun.

BENJAMIN FRANKLIN

It is only great souls
that know how much glory
there is in being good.

SOPHOCLES

If you don't know
what you want,
you're never going
to get it.

J. BUTLER

Hardening
of the heart
ages people
more quickly
than hardening
of the arteries.

FRANKLIN FIELD

There's a big
difference between
putting your nose in
other people's business
and putting your
heart in other
people's problems.

Chapter Four
The Way of Love

Love can neither be bought nor sold; its only price is love.

It requires only an ounce of grace and a thimbleful of brains to hold a grudge, but to entirely forget an injury is truly beautiful.

Scatter seeds of kindness
Everywhere you go;
Scatter bits of courtesy—
Watch them grow and grow.
Gather buds of friendship;
Keep them till full-blown;
You will find more happiness
Than you have ever known.

AMY R. RAABE

Hearts that are open to the
love that is God, feel loved in
loving and served in serving.

EDWARD GLOEGGLER

The best things in life
are never rationed.
Friendship, loyalty, love,
do not require coupons.

G. T. HEWITT

Love at Home

Home is the one place in all this world where hearts are sure of each other. It is the place of confidence. It is the place where we tear off that mask of guarded and suspicious coldness which the world forces us to wear

in self-defense, and where we pour out the unreserved communications of full and confiding hearts. It is the spot where expressions of tenderness gush out without any sensation of awkward-ness and without any dread of ridicule.

FREDERICK W. ROBERTSON

Do good
with what
thou hast
or it will
do thee
no good.

*H*e has achieved success
who has lived well,
laughed often,
and loved much.

BESSIE ANDERSON STANLEY

*K*indness gives
birth to kindness.

SOPHOCLES

Love doesn't make the
world go round. Love is what
makes the ride worthwhile.

F. P. JONES

If slighted, slight the slight,
and love the slighter.

What is life without
the radiance of love?

*W*ho has not found
the heaven below,
will fail of it above.
God's residence is
next to mine,
*H*is furniture is love.

EMILY DICKINSON

Even if it's a little thing,
do something for those who
have need of help, something
for which you get no pay
but the privilege of doing it.

ALBERT SCHWEITZER

Every charitable act is a
stepping stone toward heaven.

HENRY WARD BEECHER

Love has no thought of self!
Love sacrifices all things to
bless the thing it loves.

LORD LYTTON

Marriages are not made in
heaven. They come in kits, and
you have to put them together.

If you want to be miserable,
hate somebody.

Love Yourself

I guess it all comes down to the fact that you can't let yourself be loved, unless you love yourself. And that would make a great title for a country-western song.

RON WILSON

Life is short and we never have enough time for gladdening the hearts of those who travel the way with us. Oh, be swift to love. Make haste to be kind.

HENRI FREDERIC AMIEL

How much the wife is dearer than the bride.

LORD LYTTLETON

Wash what is dirty.

Water what is dry.

Heal what is wounded.

Warm what is cold.

Guide what goes off the road.

Love those who are least lovable
because they need it the most.

Always be a little
kinder than necessary.

JAMES M. BARRIE

CHAPTER FIVE
A Cheerful Heart

Joy is not in things, it is in us.

CHARLES WAGNER

*True happiness consists
in making happy.*

A cheerful heart spins much flax.

We miss the really great
joys of life scrambling for
bargain-counter happiness.

ROY L. SMITH

Happiness grows at our
own firesides, and is not to be
picked in strangers' gardens.

DOUGLAS JERROLD

Take time to laugh.
It is the music of the soul.

UNKNOWN

Each happiness of yesterday is
a memory for tomorrow.

GEORGE WEBSTER DOUGLAS

It is almost impossible to
smile on the outside without
feeling better on the inside.

A man without mirth
is like a wagon without springs,
he is jolted disagreeably
by every pebble in the road.

HENRY WARD BEECHER

We are all here for a spell,
get all the good laughs you can.

WILL ROGERS

A cheerful look brings joy to the heart, and good news gives health to the bones. A cheerful heart is good medicine, but a crushed spirit dries up the bones.

PROVERBS 15:30; 17:22

*D*o not put off till tomorrow what can be enjoyed today.

JOSH BILLINGS

Lose no chance
of giving pleasure.

FRANCES R. HAVERGAL

Blessed is he who has learned
to laugh at himself, for he shall
never cease to be entertained.

JOHN BOWELL

A smile is a curve that can
straighten out a lot of things.

Let us all be happy and live
within our means—even if we
have to borrow money to do it.

ARTEMUS WARD

I accept life unconditionally.
Life holds so much—so much
to be happy about always.
Happiness can be felt only
if you don't set conditions.

ARTHUR RUBENSTEIN

If you laugh a lot, when you
get older your wrinkles
will be in the right places.

As much of heaven is visible
as we have eyes to see.

WILLIAM WINTER

Happiness is not something
you get, but something you do.

The poorest
people in the world are
those who have more
than they need but feel
it isn't enough.

There is no cosmetic
for beauty like
happiness.

LADY BLESSINGTON

If you haven't
all the things you want,
be grateful for the things
you don't have that
you wouldn't want.

Enjoy your own life
without comparing it
with that of another.

I am

an optimist.

It does not seem

too much

use being

anything else.

WINSTON CHURCHILL

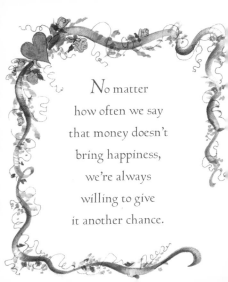

No matter
how often we say
that money doesn't
bring happiness,
we're always
willing to give
it another chance.

Never lose an
opportunity of seeing
anything that is beautiful;
for beauty is God's
handwriting—
a wayside sacrament.

RALPH WALDO EMERSON

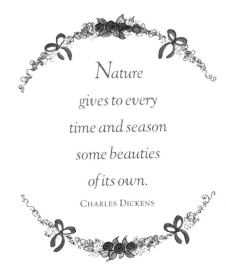

Nature

gives to every

time and season

some beauties

of its own.

CHARLES DICKENS

Most folks are
about as happy as they
make up their minds to be.

ABRAHAM LINCOLN

The only ones among you
who will be really happy are
those who will have sought
and found how to serve.

ALBERT SCHWEITZER

A smart wife has the pork chops ready when her husband comes home from a fishing trip.

All happiness is in the mind.

A rich man is one who when his pockets are empty, his children fill his arms.

*When friends are near,
hearts abound in love.*